OCS Study MMS 2006-015

Final Report

Role of Grazers on the Recolonization of Hard-Bottom Communities in the Alaska Beaufort Sea

Principal Investigator: Brenda Konar
School of Fisheries and Ocean Sciences
University of Alaska Fairbanks
bkonar@guru.uaf.edu

May 2006

Table of Contents

List of Figures

List of Tables

Abstract

Recovery and recolonization of hard-bottom macroalgal communities vary temporally and spatially because of multiple biotic and abiotic factors. This study examined the relative importance of grazing on recolonization rates of sessile organisms in a high latitude environment, the Boulder Patch in the Beaufort Sea. A simple manipulative experiment using cleared boulders and cages was used to test the hypothesis that grazing causes slow recovery of sessile macrophytic and macrofaunal communities. Monitoring cleared boulders (caged and uncaged) for three years resulted in no growth of any sessile organism for the first two years. In the third year, new invertebrate and coralline growth was seen on 79% of the cleared boulders, with significantly more growth on caged boulders. Uncleared control rocks showed no significant temporal variation. Concurrent surveys and observations suggested that in this arctic community 1) there were two conspicuous types of macrograzers on rocks, chitons and seastars, 2) space was limiting, 3) the dominant alga, *Laminaria solidungula* was reproductive during the study period. This study strongly suggests that any perturbations causing scouring of hard substrate in the Beaufort Sea will result in very slow community recovery.

Introduction

Alaska's Beaufort Sea shelf is typically characterized by silty sands and mud and as having an absence of macroalgal beds and associated organisms (Barnes and Reimnitz 1974). In 1971, a diverse kelp and invertebrate community was discovered near Prudhoe Bay in Stefansson Sound, Alaska (Figure 1). This area was named the Boulder Patch by the U.S. Board of Geographic Names. Since its discovery, the Boulder Patch has been subject to much biological and geological research (Dunton et al. 1982, Dunton and Schell 1987, Dunton and Jodwalis 1988, Dunton 1990, Martin and Gallaway 1994, MMS 1996, 1998, Dunton and Schonberg 2000, Konar and Iken 2005, and others).

The Boulder Patch contains numerous cobbles and boulders that provide substrate for attachment for many invertebrates, several species of red and brown algae, and one green alga. These algae and epilithic invertebrates cover nearly all exposed substrate, except recently upturned rocks. The invertebrate assemblage that inhabits the rocks and associated kelp beds has representatives from every major phylum (Dunton 1985). The dominant brown alga is *Laminaria solidungula*, which constitutes 90% of the brown algal biomass (Dunton et al. 1982). This alga is an important food source to many benthic and epibenthic organisms (Dunton and Schell 1987). Differences in infaunal abundance and biomass between the Boulder Patch and peripheral sediment areas demonstrate the importance of this unique habitat (Dunton and Schonberg 2000).

Boulder fields are very dynamic systems because of physical disturbance (Sousa 1979, 1980, vanTamelen 1987). In the high arctic, ice gouging can overturn large boulders and cobbles and hence expose new substrate (Dunton et al. 1982, Conlan et al. 1998). In many areas, currents can overturn smaller rocks that have epilithic organisms attached to them (Dunton et al. 1982). These organisms cause resistance to the currents, which results in rocks moving and turning. The existence of dead (white) corallines on the underside of many small rocks suggests

that these processes are common in the Boulder Patch (Dunton et al. 1982). When a boulder is overturned, algae and sessile invertebrates can be killed in whole or part by a combination of grazing, anoxia, low light levels, or mechanical damage caused by crushing or abrasion (Sousa 1980). Algal and some invertebrate populations recolonize cleared surfaces through either vegetative regrowth of surviving individuals or by recruitment from spores or larvae (Sousa 1979, Airoldi 2000).

Recolonization experiments in the Boulder Patch have shown that recovery of denuded areas is slow (Dunton et al. 1982). In temperate systems, algal communities can recover to previous densities within one year of denuding (Foster 1975, Konar and Estes 2003). Many studies on coralline algal recruitment have shown that although their growth is remarkably slow, they will settle to a visible size in a few months (Johanson and Austin 1970, Colthart and Johanson 1973, Adey and Vasser 1975, Matsuda 1989, Konar and Foster 1992, Konar 1993, Dethier and Steneck 2001). In contrast to temperate systems, 50% of the substrate in the Boulder Patch was still bare three years after an initial disturbance (Dunton et al. 1982). One reason suggested for this slow recolonization is invertebrate grazing. Motile herbivorous, omnivorous, and carnivorous invertebrates such as chitons, snails, seastars, and polychaetes have been frequently observed in the Boulder Patch (Dunton et al. 1982). Many studies have shown that grazers can be very important in structuring communities (Johnson et al. 1997, Worm and Chapman 1998, Jenkins et al. 1999, Ojeda and Munoz 1999, Morton 1999, Wilson et al. 1999, Konar 2000, and others).

The reason that grazing has been suggested to cause the slow recovery in the Boulder Patch is that polystyrene floats (suspended 1 m above the bottom) that were used to mark sites in a study by Dunton (1985) recolonized much more quickly than denuded substrates. When the floats were first examined by Dunton 12 months after initial deployment, all were covered with hydroids, bryozoans, red algae, and polychaete worm tubes. This is the same suite of species that eventually recruited onto the denuded experimental boulders; however, recruitment onto the boulders was much slower. Since the floats were not intended to be experimental substrates, no quantitative comparison was made to non-floating experimental substrates. Dunton (1985) did suggest that these floats may have recovered faster than the experimental substrates because the floats were not subject to grazing or predation pressures by benthic animals. Recruitment onto the floats may have been due to larvae and spores exhibiting a substrate preference for polystyrene; however, Dunton concluded that this was unlikely because probably not all epilithic species possess the same selectivity for this artificial substrate.

To determine if grazing is associated with the slow recruitment in the Boulder Patch, various comparisons using exclusion cages, cage controls, and natural rock were employed. The specific hypothesis tested was that there would be no significant difference between recruitment of sessile organisms on cleared boulders with and without cages, which were employed to exclude macrograzers. Concurrent with this recruitment study, community observations and surveys were performed to determine which macrograzers were the most conspicuous on the rocks, if space was limiting (which would be suggested by a paucity of bare space on rocks), and if the dominant brown alga, *Laminaria solidungula*, was reproductive during the study period.

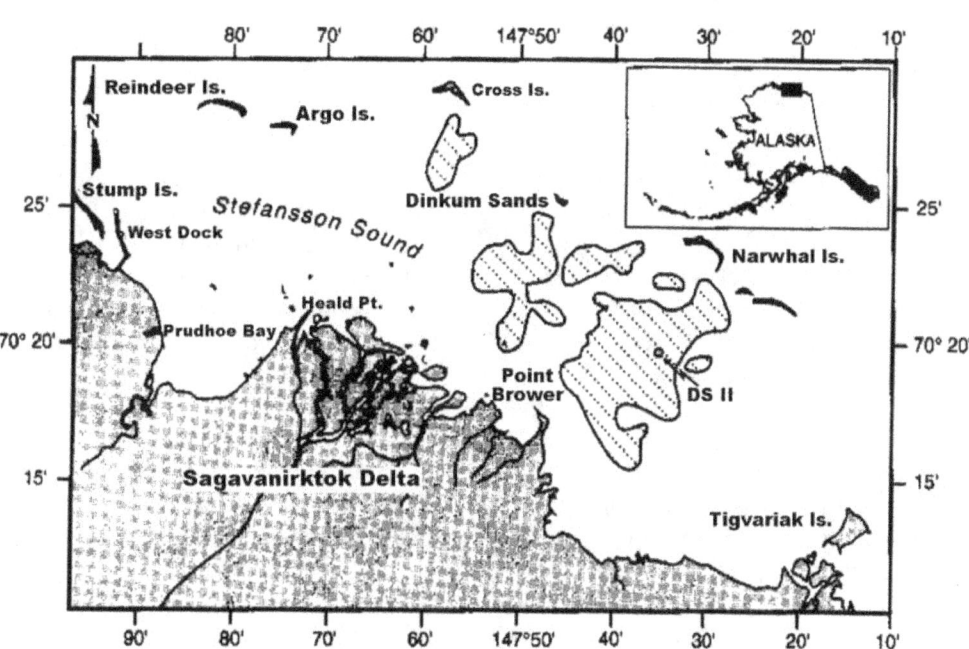

Figure 1: Chart of Stefansson Sound within the Beaufort Sea showing the location of DS11 within the Boulder Patch. Hatched polygons are areas with high boulder/cobble density. Figure from Dunton and Schonberg (2000).

Methods

Cages

To address the hypothesis that there is no significant difference between recruitment of sessile organisms on cleared boulders with and without cages, cage and non-cage treatments were deployed at each of the three sites within DS11 at the Boulder Patch in August 2002 (Figure 1). Cages are commonly used for inclusion and exclusion manipulative experiments (see Vadas 1985, Coyer et al. 1999 for overviews). The boulders used in this study were collected from DS11. Because of the difficulty in removing living material from rocky substrata underwater, all boulders were brought to the surface to be cleared. Care was given not to chip boulders so as to expose new surface because this leaching and weathering of newly exposed surfaces may affect recruitment (Dayton 1971, Reed and Foster 1984). After five days, denuded rocks (with and without cages and cage controls) were placed back into the field.

Six cages were deployed to exclude large macrograzers at each of three locations within DS11, totaling 18 cages. The cages were 25 cm on a side, 10 cm tall, with a 1 cm mesh size and constructed of stainless steel mesh (Figure 2). All cages were coated with a non-toxic antifouling compound to inhibit sessile invertebrate and algal growth (Coyer et al. 1999). Eighteen cage controls also were deployed to control for any artifacts caused by the cages, such as decreased light levels or increased sedimentation. These cage controls, which were cages with holes cut into the sides so that grazers could easily pass through them, are commonly used (Russ 1980, Breitberg 1985, Stocker 1986, and others). For comparison, 18 cleared rocks were deployed with no cages to determine natural recruitment. As a control for natural community changes, 18 non-cleared boulders also were monitored.

Visual estimates were used to determine percent cover of sessile organisms on all boulders. All algae (except for corallines) were identified to genus while all other organisms (corallines, sponges, bryozoans, hydroids and tunicates) were combined into larger taxonomic groups. Care was taken not to disturb boulders while sampling so as not to affect mobile organisms under and around the boulders (Chapman and Underwood 1996).

To determine if there was significant light reduction due to cage shading, light measurements were taken under and adjacent to cages and cage controls with a Li-Cor Model LI-185A Quantum Light Meter on three different days in 2002 (Foster et al. 1985, Ramus 1985). Light has been shown to influence algal recruitment (Reed and Foster 1984, Graham 1996, 1997, Edwards 1998, Dayton et al. 1999, Huovinen et al. 2000, Clark et al. 2004, and others) and to a limited extent invertebrate settlement (Duggins et al. 1990).

Some rocks that were cleared of sessile organisms were also surveyed for overlapping borders between organisms. These surveys were supplemented by other random rocks that were surveyed in the field to increase the sample size of organisms observed. This was done to determine the dominant competitors in the system (overgrowth at an overlapping border demonstrated a dominant competitor). The data obtained by these observations are presented in the appendix as a note as published by Polar Biology (Appendix 1).

Community surveys

Surveys were conducted in 2004 to determine community composition (grazers, sessile organisms, macroalgae, and bare rock), and reproductive status of the dominant alga, *Laminaria solidungula* at DS11. To determine potential grazers, random boulders were collected from fifteen $0.25m^2$ quadrats from which grazer densities were calculated. Percent cover estimates of sessile organisms (invertebrates and macroalgae) and of bare rock were used to assess substrate cover and available open space along eight randomly placed transects. Along each transect, five one-meter long random point contact bars (similar to that described by Foster 1975, Coyer et al. 1999) were randomly placed. These bars had a string attached at each end, with five knots along their length. Knots randomly placed on the line were pulled tight away from the bar and placed on the substrate, and the identity of the alga or invertebrate was recorded. If no organism was present at the knot, the type of substratum was noted. By moving the string from one side of the bar to the other, 10 points were sampled per area. Macroalgal biomass estimates were completed by collecting boulders from five randomly placed 0.25m² quadrats. Boulders were brought back to the lab where all macroalgae were removed, identified, and weighed for damp biomass. To determine if the dominant alga, *Laminaria solidungula* was reproductive at DS11, one random 10m² area was surveyed along eleven randomly placed 30m transects. All *L. solidungula* in each area were enumerated and the state of reproduction was recorded.

Cages

Community composition on the uncleared control boulders did not significantly vary over time (ANOVA, $F_{3,59}$=0.626, p=0.6, Figure 2). The majority of these uncleared boulders were covered with encrusting coralline algae and foliose algae, while very little (a mean of 2% or less) was bare. Foliose algae were primarily *Phycodrys rubens*, averaging 21% over the three year period. Other foliose algae included *Phyllophora truncata* (synonym *Coccotylus truncates*), *Dilsea socialis*, and *Odonthalia dentata*

In the first two years of this study, no growth was observed on any experimentally cleared rock. In the third year, 79% of the cleared rocks showed some growth. While growth was limited on all cleared rocks (never exceeding 10% and averaging less than 2%), the rocks in full cages had significantly more growth than the other two treatments (cage control and uncaged; ANOVA, $F_{2,39}$=10.599, p=0.0002). All growth seen in the third year was relatively small in size (typically less than 0.5cm) and included bryozoans, hydroids, spirorbids, barnacles, sponges, and encrusting corallines (Figure 3). No growth of brown or red foliose algae was seen on any cleared boulder in any year.

Cages and boulders were examined for light effects. While boulders in open areas did receive significantly more light than boulders in cages and in cage controls (ANOVA, $F_{2,6}$=12.924, p=0.0067), there was no significant light difference between cages and cage controls (Figure 4). This suggests that differences found between recruitment occurring within caged boulders and cage control boulders were not due to a lighting effect.

Community surveys

Grazers that were found in the DS11 surveys consisted of two chitons, *Amicula vistita* and *Ischnochiton albus*, and seastars of various genera (Figure 5). There were significantly more *I. albus* than there were seastars (ANOVA, $F_{2,24}$=3.264, p=0.01) but no differences were

seen between *A. vistita* densities and densities of the other two grazers during this survey.

In general, substrate (as measured by percent cover) at DS11 was dominated by encrusting corallines (Figure 6). Red holdfasts were also fairly abundant, covering approximately 25% of the substrate. Bare rock was found during these surveys, however it was in very small amounts (typically less than 5%). Overall, significant differences were found in the percent cover of various sessile organisms (ANOVA, $F_{5,234}$=103.893, p<0.0001). In particular, macroalgae were always significantly more abundant than any invertebrate group, with encrusting corallines also being more abundant than red holdfasts (Table 1).

Macroalgal biomass at DS11 in 2004 was dominated by foliose red algae, particularly *Phycodrys rubens*, *Phyllophora truncata*, and *Dilsea socialis* (Figure 7). Other reds found in these surveys included *Odonthalia dentata*, *Rhodomela confervoides*, and *Ahnfeltia* sp. Brown macroalgal biomass was dominated by *Laminaria solidungula*. *Laminaria saccharina* also was found, but in very small amounts. Another brown macroalga, *Alaria esculenta*, was not found during these surveys but was seen adjacent to some transects. Overall, some significant differences were found among the macroalgae for biomass (ANOVA, $F_{7,32}$=2.013, p=0.0841, Table 2). These differences typically involved *Phycodrys* and *Phyllophora* being significantly more abundant than other macroalgae.

Laminaria solidungula were reproductive during this study. Divers noticed this alga in a reproductive state during all years, and a quantitative survey was completed in 2004. From this survey, 115 plants out of 178 observed were reproductive, approximately 70% of the population.

Discussion

Grazing does have significant impacts on community structure and recruitment in many temperate systems. In some areas, grazers, such as urchins, can completely eliminate all foliose macroalgae and sessile invertebrates leaving a "barren ground", or encrusting coralline monoculture (Harrold and Reed 1985, Scheibling 1986, Konar and Estes 2003, and many others). In these situations, typically some event causes grazer densities to increase dramatically, such as the elimination of their top predator (see Estes et al. 1998 for example). In this study of a high latitude macroalgal community, cages that excluded macrograzers were found to have statistically significant effects on the recovery and recruitment of epilithic organisms (Figure 3). It should be noted that overall recruitment was extremely low (less than 10% on all rocks) but corallines, hydroids, and barnacles had a higher degree of presence on caged rocks than uncaged or cage control rocks.

Light effects caused by cages are probably not the reason for the differences seen on the cleared rocks. While cages placed in hard bottom communities can have artifacts such as the reduction of light and water motion affecting larval settlement of barnacles and ascidians (Schmidt and Warner 1984) and the attraction of small fish (Stocker 1986), many intertidal and subtidal studies have successfully used cages (Menge 1978, Andrew and Choat 1982, Petraitis 1983, Zeller 1988, Kennelly 1991, Williams 1993, Bartol et al. 1999, Bertness et al. 1999, Fernandes et al. 1999, Leonard 1999, and others). In this study, light reduction was noted in cages (Figure 4), however, no differences in light were found between cages and cage controls. This suggests that differences seen in the results between cages and cage controls were not due to light.

Three noteworthy results from this study were: First, from the community surveys of sessile organisms (percent cover–Figure 6 and biomass estimates–Figure 7) and surveys of control rocks (Figure 2), the dominant organisms in this high latitude community are the encrusting corallines (by percent cover) and the red and brown macroalgae (by biomass). In fact, the monitoring surveys of the uncleared control rocks demonstrated that the composition of this community is very stable as no significant temporal variation was noted. Interestingly, no foliose red or brown macroalgal individuals

recruited to any cleared rock in three years of monitoring. Typically, exclusion of grazers causes an increase in foliose macroalgae (Belliveau and Paul 2002). Along with the lack of foliose macroalgal recruitment, encrusting coralline recruitment also was very limited, found only on one caged boulder. In other studies, these algal organisms, particularly corallines, have been amongst the first to colonize and do so relatively quickly (Konar and Foster 1992, Airoldi 2000). While the reproductive status of the corallines was not assessed during this study, the dominant brown macroalga, *Laminaria solidungula*, was observed to be reproductive during all years. Reproductive status of this alga was quantified in 2004 and these surveys showed that approximately 70% of the plants were reproductive. Reproductive maturity of one red alga, *Phyllophora truncata*, was observed in multiple years as many of these plants contained cystocarpic material (pers. obs.). The reasons why these reproductive macroalgae were not recruiting onto the cleared areas are unknown and can only be speculated. Macroalgae are known to have recruitment "windows" where specific conditions are needed for sexual propagules to establish, whereas vegetative propagation is much more constant and predictable (Deysher and Dean 1986, Airoldi 2000). In this study, rocks were completely cleared so vegetative regrowth was not possible. Perhaps much of the recovery that occurs in this system is accomplished through regrowth and not recruitment. Boulder Patch sessile organisms do compete for space through vegetative growth as seen by overlapping borders of existing organisms (Konar and Iken 2005). The rate of growth and subsequent recovery from disturbances are unknown and require further investigation.

The second noteworthy result was that barnacles were among the dominant space occupiers on cleared boulders (especially in the cages). This is contrary to another study that found that barnacles recruited less inside cages than outside, which was speculated to have been caused by reduced light and water motion (Schmidt and Warner 1984). In the Boulder Patch, community surveys based on percent cover and surveys of uncleared control rocks never resulted in barnacle presence. In fact, sessile invertebrates actually appear to play a minor role (typically less than 10%) as far as space occupation (based on percent cover as biomass was not recorded for invertebrates in this study). One potential reason for the presence of barnacles on the cleared rocks but not in the community surveys is that the barnacles that were found were extremely small, typically less that 2mm. Organisms this small would be missed in community surveys because of the overwhelming dominance of other organisms. Perhaps multiple very small (but reproductive) barnacles inhabit the community, but they rarely grow to significant size.

The third and most noteworthy result of this study is the extremely slow recolonization rate. As in many other macroalgal systems, surveys in this study suggest that available substrate is a limiting resource in the Boulder Patch. Very little bare rock was found during the community surveys (Figure 6). Observations of these rocks showed that most had no bare space and that only a few had a bit more (but never exceeding about 10%). Ecological theory asserts that if space becomes available in a space limiting system, recruitment onto these bare areas should be rapid (Castro and Huber 2005). In a clearing experiment at a subtidal site in California, it took only a few weeks for coralline recruits to be visible to the naked eye (Foster 1975, Konar and Foster 1992). In Kachemak Bay Alaska, subtidal recruits began to settle on cleared rocks after just a couple months (Harman and Konar, unpublished data). Typically, one to two years after clearing, bare areas can not be distinguished from control areas (Foster 1975, Konar and Foster 1992, Konar and Estes 2003). At the current recruitment rate in the Boulder Patch, it might take 10+ years for full recovery if rocks are completely damaged and vegetative regrowth is not possible. The reasons for this incredibly slow recruitment in the Boulder Patch are unknown. Also, the actual time that would be needed for a full recovery is unknown. Both the reason for the slow recovery and the time needed for a full recovery require more study and are imperative knowledge that should be obtained if the Boulder Patch is to be preserved. This study strongly suggests that any perturbations causing scouring of hard substrate in the Beaufort Sea will result in very slow community recovery.

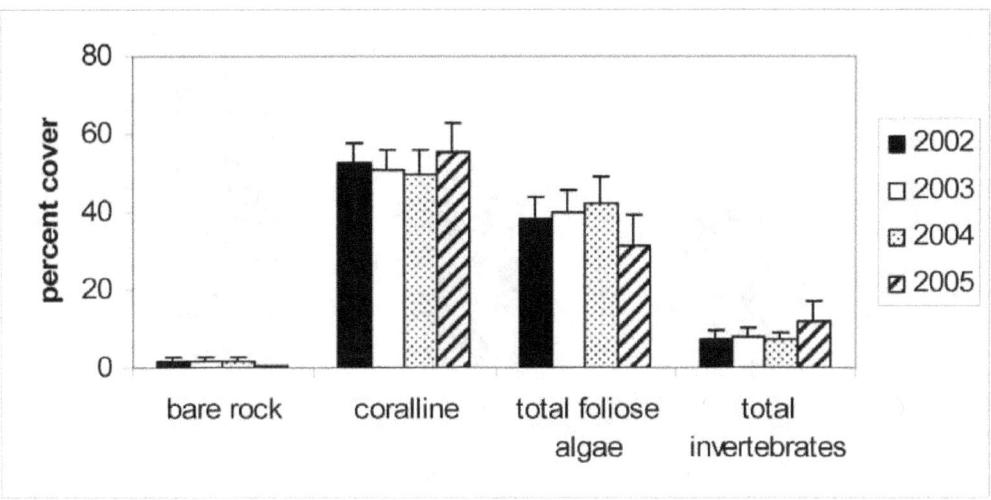

Figure 2: Mean percent cover (±1 s.e.) of bare rock, encrusting coralline algae, total foliose algae, and total invertebrates on uncleared control boulders in 2002 through 2005. n=18, 18, 15, and 12 for 2002, 2003, 2004, and 2005, respectively.

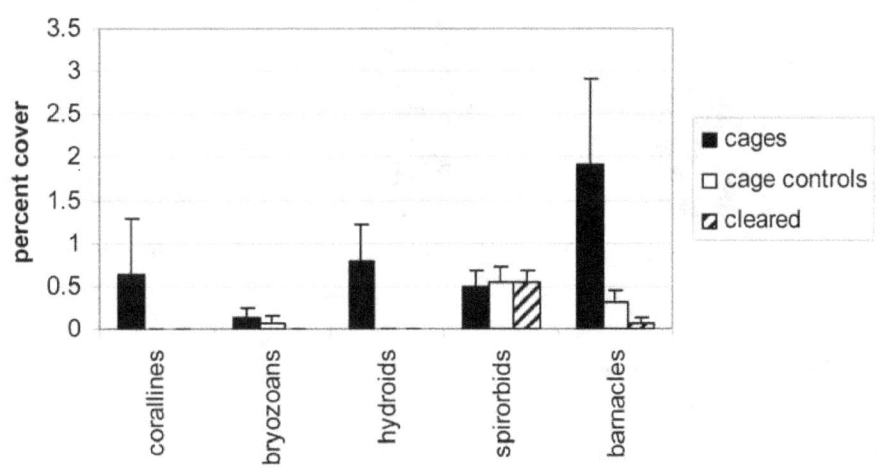

Figure 3: Mean percent cover (±1 s.e.) of encrusting coralline algae, bryozoans, hydroids, spirorbids, and barnacles on each of the treatment boulders in 2005. n=14, 13, and 15 for cages, cage controls, and cleared rocks, respectively.

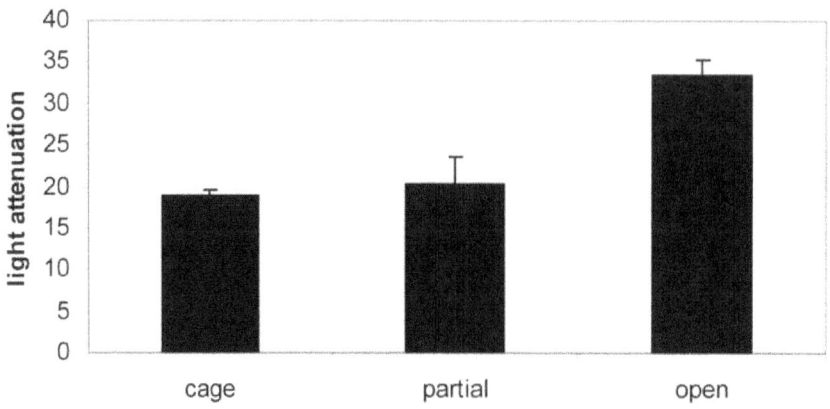

Figure 4: Mean percent light attenuation (±1 s.e.) under cages, in cage controls, and adjacent to cages. Measurements were taken on three separate days in 2002.

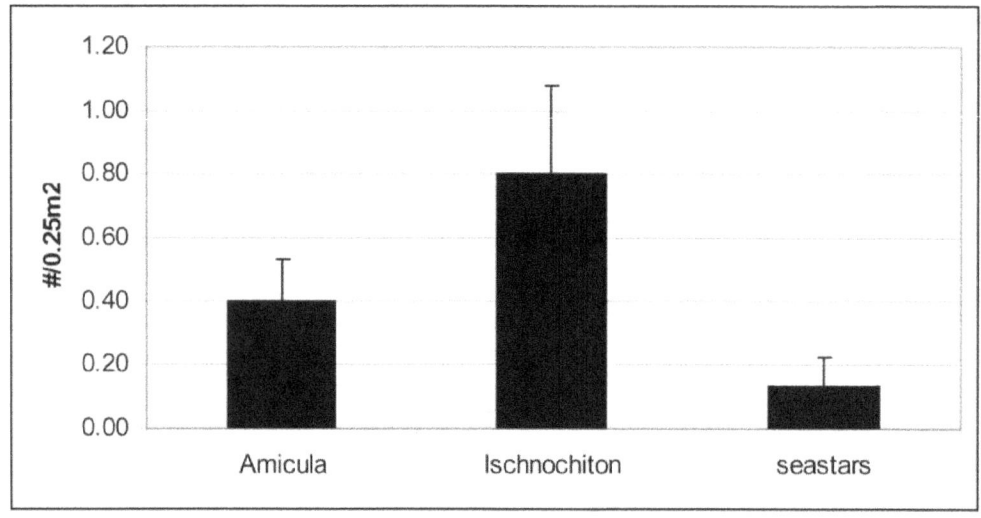

Figure 5: Mean density (±1 s.e.) of grazers at DS11 in 2004. Estimates are from searches done on fifteen randomly placed 0.25m^2 quadrats.

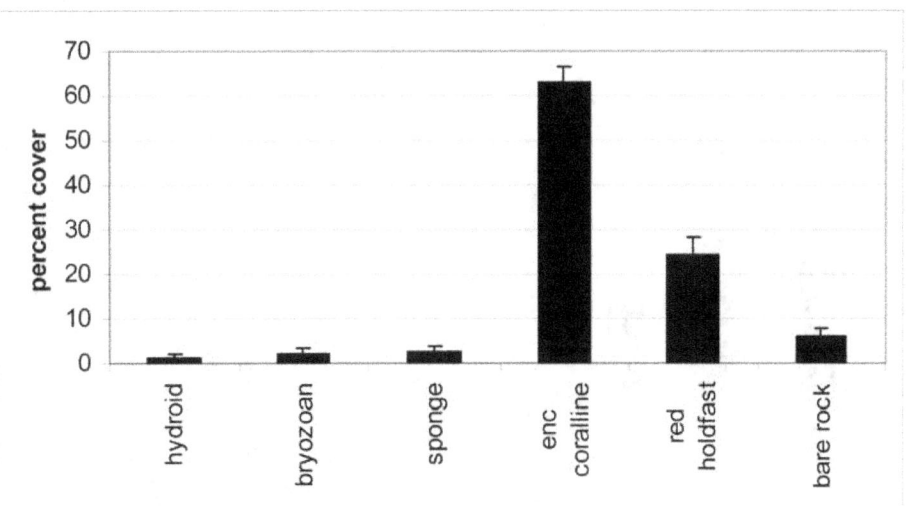

Figure 6: Percent cover (±1 s.e.) of sessile organisms and bare rock at DS11 in 2004. Estimates are from five random point contacts placed along eight randomly placed transects.

Table 1: Fisher's PLSD for percent cover of sessile organisms and bare rock at DS11 in 2004. S=Significance level of 5%.

	Mean Diff.	Crit. Diff.	P-Value	
hydroid, bryozoan	-.843	6.623	.8021	
hydroid, sponge	-1.235	6.623	.7136	
hydroid, red holdfast	-23.030	6.623	<.0001	S
hydroid, encrusting coralline	-61.340	6.623	<.0001	S
hydroid, bare rock	-4.593	6.623	.1731	
bryozoan, sponge	-.392	6.623	.9073	
bryozoan, red holdfast	-22.186	6.623	<.0001	S
bryozoan, encrusting coralline	-60.497	6.623	<.0001	S
bryozoan, bare rock	-3.750	6.623	.2658	
sponge, red holdfast	-21.794	6.623	<.0001	S
sponge, encrusting coralline	-60.105	6.623	<.0001	S
sponge, bare rock	-3.358	6.623	.3188	
red holdfast, encrusting coralline	-38.311	6.623	<.0001	S
red holdfast, bare rock	18.436	6.623	<.0001	S
encrusting coralline, bare rock	56.747	6.623	<.0001	S

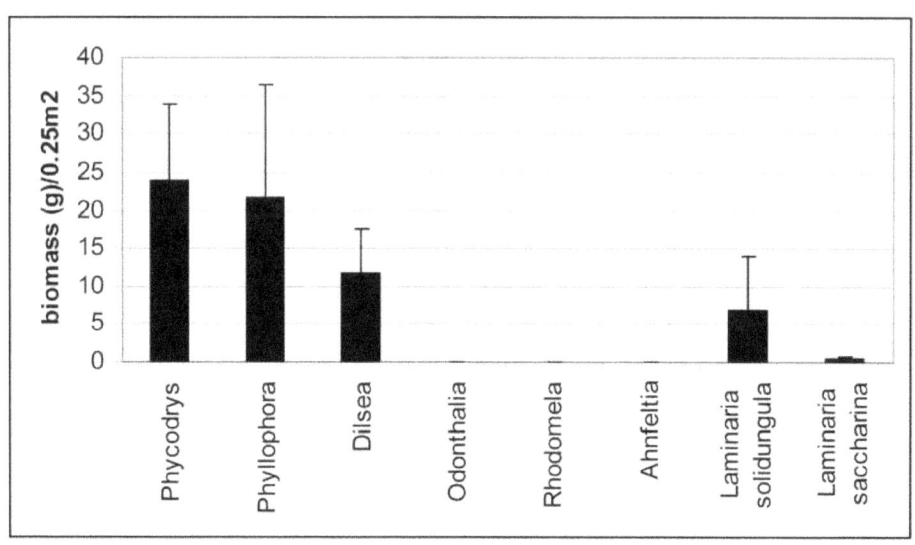

Figure 7: Biomass (±1 s.e.) in grams of macroalgae at DS11 in 2004. Estimates are from five 0.25m^2 randomly placed quadrats.

	Mean Diff.	Crit. Diff.	P-Value	
Phycodrys, Phyllophora	2.420	20.397	.8106	
Phycodrys, Dilsea	12.240	20.397	.2305	
Phycodrys, Odonthalia	24.000	20.397	.0226	S
Phycodrys, Rhodomela	24.020	20.397	.0224	S
Phycodrys, Ahnfeltia	24.020	20.397	.0224	S
Phycodrys, L. solidungula	17.040	20.397	.0985	
Phycodrys, L. saccharina	23.640	20.397	.0245	S
Phyllophora, Dilsea	9.820	20.397	.3341	
Phyllophora, Odonthalia	21.580	20.397	.0388	S
Phyllophora, Rhodomela	21.600	20.397	.0386	S
Phyllophora, Ahnfeltia	21.600	20.397	.0386	S
Phyllophora, L. solidungula	14.620	20.397	.1540	
Phyllophora, L. saccharina	21.220	20.397	.0419	S
Dilsea, Odonthalia	11.760	20.397	.2489	
Dilsea, Rhodomela	11.780	20.397	.2481	
Dilsea, Ahnfeltia	11.780	20.397	.2481	
Dilsea, L. solidungula	4.800	20.397	.6349	
Dilsea, L. saccharina	11.400	20.397	.2634	
Odonthalia, Rhodomela	.020	20.397	.9984	
Odonthalia, Ahnfeltia	.020	20.397	.9984	
Odonthalia, L. solidungula	-6.960	20.397	.4920	
Odonthalia, L. saccharina	-.360	20.397	.9715	
Rhodomela, Ahnfeltia	0.000	20.397	.	
Rhodomela, L. solidungula	-6.980	20.397	.4908	
Rhodomela, L. saccharina	-.380	20.397	.9700	
Ahnfeltia, L. solidungula	-6.980	20.397	.4908	
Ahnfeltia, L. saccharina	-.380	20.397	.9700	
L. solidungula, L. saccharina	6.600	20.397	.5145	

Table 2: Fisher's PLSD for macroalgal biomass at DS11 in 2004. S=Significance level of 5%.

Acknowledgements

This project could not have been completed without the logistical support offered by the Dunton Brothers and by BP (particularly everyone at Endicott Production Island). I also would like to thank my field assistants: Katrin Iken, Casey Debenham, Nicholas Harman, and Chris Wyatt. Ken Dunton guided many stimulating discussions on Boulder Patch biology. Katrin Iken provided insightful advice during this study and on the manuscript. This project was partially funded by the Coastal Marine Institute. Match support was provided by BP.

Study Products

Refereed Publications

Konar, B and K Iken. 2005. Competitive dominance among sessile marine organisms in a high Arctic boulder community. Polar Biology. (see Appendix 1)

Technical Reports

Role of grazers in the recolonization of hard-bottom communities in the Alaska Beaufort Sea. Annual Reports for 2003 and 2004.

Presentations and Interviews

March 8, 2005: Presentation at Coastal Marine Institute Annual Meeting

February 16, 2004: Presentation at Coastal Marine Institute Annual Meeting

November 7–10, 2003: Symposium Speaker: Western Society of Naturalists, 84th Annual Meeting in Long Beach, CA

August 22, 2003: Interviewed for KUAC on Boulder Patch project

August 10, 2003: Presentation for Endicott Island BP workers

August 5, 2003: Interviewed for series on Boulder Patch project for KUAC

February 19, 2003: Presentation at Coastal Marine Institute Annual Meeting

November 8–11, 2002: Poster presented at the Western Society of Naturalists 83rd Annual Meeting in Monterey, CA

October 2002: Interviewed by Arctic Science Journeys radio program

August 1 and 8, 2002: Presentation for Endicott Island BP workers

November 18–20, 2005, Western Society of Naturalists 86th Annual Meeting in Monterey, CA, Symposium Speaker

References

Adey, W. H. and J. M. Vasser, 1975. Colonization, succession and growth rates of tropical crustose coralline algae (Rhodophyta, Cryptonemiales). Phycologia 14:55–69.

Airoldi, L. 2000. Responses of algae with different life histories to temporal and spatial variability of disturbance in subtidal. Marine Ecology Progress Series 195:81–92.

Andrew, N. L. and J. H. Choat. 1982. The influence of predation and conspecific adults on the abundance of juvenile *Evechinus chloroticus* (Echinoidea: Echinodermetridae). Oecolgia 54:80–87.

Barnes, P. W. and E. Reimnitz. 1974. Sedimentary processes on arctic shelves off the northern coast of Alaska: *In:* Reed, J. and J. E. Slater (eds.). The Coast and Shelf of the Beaufort Sea, Arlington, VA: Arctic Institute of North America. Pp. 439–476.

Bartol, I. K., R. Mann and M. Luckenbach. 1999. Growth and mortality of oysters (*Crassostrea virginica*) on constructed intertidal reefs: effects of tidal height and substrate level. Journal of Experimental Marine Biology and Ecology 237:157–184.

Belliveau, S. A and V. J. Paul. 2002. Effects of herbivory and nutrients on the early colonization of crustose coralline and fleshy algae. Marine Ecology Progress Series 232:105–114.

Bertness, M. D., G. H. Leonard, J. M. Levine, P. R. Schmidt and A. O. Ingraham. 1999. Testing the relative contribution of positive and negative interactions in rocky intertidal communities. Ecology 80:2711–2726.

Breitburg, D. L. 1985. Development of a subtidal epibenthic community: factors affecting species composition and the mechanisms of succession. Oecologia 65:173–184,

Castro, P. and M. Huber. 2005. Marine Biology, 5th edition. McGraw–Hill Companies Inc.

Chapman, M. G. and A. J. Underwood. 1996. Experiments on effects of sampling biota under intertidal and shallow subtidal boulders. Journal of Experimental Marine Biology and Ecology 207:103–126.

Clark, R. P., M. S. Edwards and M. S. Foster. 2004. Effects of shade from multiple kelp canopies on an understory algal assemblage. Marine Ecology Progress Series 267:107–119.

Colthart, B. J. and H. W. Johanson. 1973. Growth rates of *Corallina officianalis* (Rhodophyta) at different temperatures. Marine Biology 18:46–49.

Conlan, K. E., H. S. Lenihan, R. G. Kvitek and J. S. Oliver. 1998. Ice scour disturbance to benthic communities in the Canadian High Arctic. Marine Ecology Progress Series 166:1–16.

Coyer, J., D. Steller and J. Witman. 1999. A Guide to Methods in Underwater Research: The Underwater Catalog. Shoals Marine Laboratory.

Dayton, P. K. 1971. Competition, disturbance, and community organization: the provision and subsequent utilization of space in a rocky intertidal community. Ecological Monographs 41:351–389.

Dayton, P. K., M. J. Tegner, P. B. Edwards and K. L. Riser. 1999. Temporal and spatial scales of kelp demography: the role of oceanographic climate. Ecological Monographs 69:219–250.

Dethier, M. N. and R. S. Steneck. 2001. Growth and persistence of diverse intertidal crusts: survival of the slow in a fast-paced world, Marine Ecology Progress Series 223: 89–100.

Deysher, L. E. and T. A. Dean. 1986. *In situ* recruitment of sporophytes of the giant kelp, *Macrocystis pyrifera* (L.) C. A. Agardh: effects of physical factors. Journal of Experimental Marine Biology and Ecology 103:41–63.

Duggins, D. O., J. E. Eckman and A. T. Sewell. 1990. Ecology of understory kelp environments. 2. Effects of kelps on recruitment of benthic invertebrates. Journal of Experimental Marine Biology and Ecology 143:27–45.

Dunton, K. H. 1985. Trophic dynamics in marine nearshore systems of the Alaskan high arctic. PhD Dissertation. University of Alaska Fairbanks.

Dunton, K.H. 1990. Growth and production in *Laminaria solidungula*: relation to continuous underwater light levels in the Alaskan High Arctic. Marine Biology 106:297–304.

Dunton, K. H. and C. M. Jodwalis. 1988. Photosynthetic performance of *Laminaria solidungula* measured *in situ* in the Alaskan High Arctic. Marine Biology 98:277–285.

Dunton, K. H. and D. M. Schell. 1987. Dependence of consumers on macroalgal (*Laminaria solidungula*) carbon in an arctic kelp community: δ13C evidence. Marine Biology 93:615–625.

Dunton, K. H. and S. V. Schonberg. 2000. The benthic faunal assemblage of the Boulder Patch kelp community, Chapter 18. *In:* The Natural History of an Arctic Oil Field. Academic Press.

Dunton, K. H., E. Reimnitz and S. Schonberg. 1982. An Arctic kelp community in the Alaskan Beaufort Sea. Arctic 35:465–484.

Estes, J. A., M. T. Tinker, T. M. Williams and D. F. Doak. 1998. Killer whale predation on sea otters linking oceanic and nearshore ecosystems. Science 282:473–476.

Edwards, M. S. 1998. Effects of long-term kelp canopy exclusion on the abundance of the annual alga *Desmarestia ligulata* (Light F). Journal of Experimental Marine Biology and Ecology 228:309–326.

Fernandes, T. F., M. Huxham and S. R. Piper. 1999. Predator caging experiments: a test of the importance of scale. Journal of Experimental Marine Biology and Ecology 241:137–154.

Foster, M. S. 1975. Algal succession in a Macrocystis pyrifera forest. Marine Biology 32:313–329.

Foster, M. S., T. A. Dean, and L. E. Deysher. 1985. Subtidal techniques. *In:* Littler, M. M. and D. S. Littler (eds.). Handbook of Phycological Methods, Ecological Field Methods: Macroalgae pp. 199–232.

Graham, M. H. 1996. Effect of irradiance on recruitment of the giant kelp *Macrocystis* (Phaeophyta) in shallow water. Journal of Phycology 32:903–906.

Graham, M. H. 1997. Factors determining the upper limit of giant kelp, *Macrocystis pyrifera* Agardh, along Monterey Peninsula, central California, USA. Journal of Experimental Marine Biology and Ecology 218:127–149.

Harrold, C. and D. C. Reed. 1985. Food availability, sea urchin grazing, and kelp forest community structure. Ecology 66:1160–1169.

Huovinen, P. S., A. O. J. Oikari, M. R. Soimasuo and G. N. Cherr. 2000. Impact of UV radiation on the early development of the giant kelp (*Macrocystis pyrifera*) gametophytes. Photochemistry and Photobiology 72:308–313.

Jenkins, S. R., S. J. Hawkins and T. A. Norton. 1999. Interaction between a fucoid canopy and limpet grazing in structuring a low shore intertidal community. Journal of Experimental Marine Biology and Ecology 233:41–63.

Johanson, H. W. and L. F. Austin. 1970. Growth rates in the articulated coralline *Calliarthron* (Rhodophyta). Can. J. Bot. 48:25–132.

Johnson M. P., M. T. Burrows, R. G. Hartnoll and S. J. Hawkins. 1997. Spatial structure on moderately exposed rocky shores: Patch scales and the interactions between limpets and algae. Marine Ecology Progress Series 160:209–215.

Kennelly, S. J. 1991. Caging experiments to examine the effects of fishes on understory species in a sublittoral kelp community. Journal of Experimental Marine Biology and Ecology 147:207–230.

Konar, B. 2000. Seasonal inhibitory effects of marine plants on sea urchins: structuring communities the algal way. Oecologia 125:208–217.

Konar, B. 1993. Demography and morphology of the geniculate coralline, *Bossiella californica* ssp. *schmittii* (Corallinales, Rhodophyta), in a central California kelp forest. Phycologia 32:284–290.

Konar B. and J. A. Estes. 2003. The stability of boundary regions between kelp beds and deforested areas. Ecology 84:174–185.

Konar, B. and M. S. Foster. 1992. Distribution and recruitment of subtidal geniculate coralline algae. Journal of Phycology 28:273–280.

Konar, B. and K. Iken. 2005. Competitive dominance among sessile marine organisms in a high Arctic boulder community. Polar Biology.

Leonard, G. H. 1999. Positive and negative effects of intertidal algal canopies on recruitment and survival of barnacles. Marine Ecology Progress Series 178:241–249.

Martin, L. R. and B. J. Gallaway. 1994. The effects of the Endicott Development Project on the Boulder Patch, an Arctic kelp community in Stefansson Sound, Alaska. Arctic 47:54–64.

Matsuda, S. 1989. Succession and growth rates of encrusting crustose coralline algae (Rhodophyta, Cryptonemiales) in the upper fore-reef environment off Ishigaki Island, Ryukyu Islands. Coral Reefs 7:185–195.

Menge, B. A. 1978. Predation intensity in a rocky intertidal community. Effect of an algal canopy, wave action and desiccation on predator feeding rates. Oecologia 34:17–35.

Minerals Management Service. 1996. Beaufort Sea planning area oil and gas lease sale 144. Final Environmental Impact Statement. MMS OCS EIS/EA MMS 96-0012. U.S. Dept. of Interior, MMS, Alaska Outer Continental Shelf Region, Anchorage, Alaska.

Minerals Management Service. 1998. Arctic Kelp Workshop Proceedings, Anchorage Alaska. T. Newbury (ed) OCS Study MMS 98-0038. U.S. Dept. of Interior, MMS, Alaska Outer Continental Shelf Region, Anchorage, Alaska.

Morton, B. 1999. Competitive grazers and the predatory whelk *Lepsiella flindersi* (Gastropoda: Muricidae) structure a mussel bed (*Xenostrobus pulex*) on a southwest Australian shore. Journal of Molluscan Studies 65:435–452.

Ojeda, F. P. and A. A. Munoz. 1999. Feeding selectivity of the herbivorous fish *Scartichthys viridis*: effects on macroalgal community structure in a temperate rocky intertidal coastal zone. Marine Ecology Progress Series 184:219–229.

Petraitis, P. S. 1983. Grazing patterns of the periwinkle and their effect in sessile intertidal organisms. Ecology 64:522–533.

Ramus, J. 1985. Light. *In:* Littler, M. M. and D. S. Littler (eds.) Handbook of Phycological Methods. Ecological Field Methods: Macroalgae. Cambridge University Press.

Reed, D. C. and M. S. Foster. 1984. The effects of canopy shading on algal recruitment and growth in a giant kelp forest. Ecology 65:937–948.

Russ, G. R. 1980. Effects of predation by fishes, competition, and structural complexity of the substratum on the establishment of a marine epifaunal community. Journal of Experimental Biology and Ecology 42:55–69.

Scheibling, R. 1986. Increased macroalgal abundance following mass mortalities of sea urchins (*Strongylocentrotus droebachiensis*) along the Atlantic coast of Nova Scotia. Oecologia 68:186–198.

Schmidt, G. H. and G. F. Warner. 1984. Effects of caging on the development of a sessile epifaunal community. Marine Ecology Progress Series 15:251–263.

Sousa, W. P. 1979. Experimental investigations of disturbance and ecological succession in a rocky intertidal algal community. Ecological Monographs 49:227–254.

Sousa, W. P. 1980. The responses of a community to disturbance: the importance of successional age and species' life histories. Oecologia 45:72–81.

Stocker, L. J. 1986. Artifactual effects of caging on the recruitment and survivorship of a subtidal colonial invertebrate. Marine Ecology Progress Series 34:305–307.

Vadas, R. L. 1985. Herbivory. *In:* Littler, M. M. and D. S. Littler (eds.). Handbook of Phycological Methods, Ecological Field Methods: Macroalgae 531–572.

vanTamelen, P. G. 1987. Early successional mechanisms in the rocky intertidal: the role of direct and indirect interaction. Journal of Experimental Marine Biology and Ecology 112:39–48.

Williams, G. A. 1993. Seasonal variation in algal species richness and abundance in the presence of molluscan herbivores on a tropical rocky shore. Journal of Experimental Marine Biology and Ecology 167:261–275.

Wilson, W. G., C. W. Osenberg, R. J. Schmitt and R. M. Nisbet. 1999. Complementary foraging behaviors allow coexistence of two consumers. Ecology 80:2358–2372.

Worm, B. and A. R. Chapman. 1998. Relative effects of elevated grazing pressure and competition from a red algal turf on two post-settlement stages of *Fucus evanescens* C. Ag. Journal of Experimental Marine Biology and Ecology 220:247–268.

Zeller, D. C. 1988. Short-term effects of territoriality of a tropical damselfish and experimental exclusion of large fishes on invertebrates in algal turfs. Marine Ecology Progress Series 44:85–93.

Appendix 1

Polar Biol (2005) 29: 61–64
DOI 10.1007/s00300-005-0055-8

SHORT NOTE

Brenda Konar · Katrin Iken

Competitive dominance among sessile marine organisms in a high Arctic boulder community

Received: 10 March 2005 / Revised: 31 July 2005 / Accepted: 5 August 2005 / Published online: 22 September 2005
© Springer-Verlag 2005

Abstract In most hard substrate environments, space is a limiting resource for sessile organisms. Competition for space is often high and is a structuring force within the community. In the Beaufort Sea's Boulder Patch, crustose coralline red algae are major space occupiers. This research determined if coralline algae were competitively dominant over other sessile organisms. To test this hypothesis, overgrowth was documented in terms of "winners" and "losers" on the contact borders between different species. Crustose corallines occurred in over 80% of the observed interactions but were only winners in approximately half of them. Most frequently, bryozoans, tunicates, and sponges were superior competitors over crustose corallines, while at the same time these invertebrate groups were among the least abundant space occupiers.

Introduction

Coexistence of species is largely driven by an interacting system of disturbance and competition (Airoldi 2000). While disturbances clear space, competitive success ultimately determines who inhabits the space. Competition for space is a major structuring force in marine benthic communities (Bertness and Leonard 1997). Substrate competition by encrusting marine organisms usually occurs by direct overgrowth at their contact zones (Sebens 1986). These competitive border interactions are commonly evaluated with species being ranked as winners or losers based on their abilities to overgrow the competing taxa. Although losers of interactions are overgrown by winners, this does not always result in

death of the overgrown organism (Jompa and McCook 2002). Coralline algae, in particular, can survive while they are overgrown and sometimes even continue to grow (Sebens 1986; Dethier and Steneck 2001). While the outcome of border interactions can vary depending on species, depth, timing, and location, some taxa are typically competitively dominant over others (Nandakumar 1996; Airoldi 2000; Barnes and Dick 2000; Barnes 2002). In temperate and polar waters, ascideans, sponges, and bryozoans have been shown to be strong space competitors (Nandakumar 1996; Maughan and Barnes 2000; Barnes and Kuklinski 2004).

The Boulder Patch is an isolated hard-bottom kelp community surrounded by the soft sediment habitat of the high Arctic Beaufort Sea. Space seems to be a limiting resource as most rock substrate is covered by sessile organisms, usually crustose coralline algae. Based on these observations, we tested whether crustose coralline algae were competitively dominant over other sessile species, and thus excluded or diminished other space occupiers. We included upright and crustose organisms in this analysis as both are space occupiers in this system. Our objectives were to determine (1) if space was limiting, (2) the dominant space occupier, and (3) which taxa were dominant competitors.

Study site

This study was conducted at the Boulder Patch in Stefansson Sound, Beaufort Sea Patch (147°40'W, 70°20'N; see Dunton 1990 for map details). Sediment load is high in this area because of run-off from the Sagavanirktok Delta, but overall sediment accumulation in the benthos is limited due to strong currents (Dunton and Schonberg 2000). Light intensity and duration for the benthic community can be reduced due to water column sediments and the polar winter, respectively (Dunton 1990). Ice scour is relatively low because the area is protected from thicker ice by offshore barrier islands. Water temperatures range from −1.9°C during

B. Konar (✉) · K. Iken
School of Fisheries and Ocean Sciences, University of Alaska
Fairbanks, Fairbanks, AK 99775-7220, USA
E-mail: bkonar@guru.uaf.edu
Tel.: +1-907-4745028
Fax: +1-907-4745804

winter to 7°C in summer. The study area was in 6–7 m water depth and contained numerous cobbles and boulders that provided substrate for several invertebrate and macroalgal species. Approximately 148 animal taxa and ten algal species are reported from the area at densities approaching 18,441 individuals/m² with a biomass of 283 g/m² (Dunton and Schonberg 2000).

Methods

To compare the availability of bare substrate to substrate covered by sessile organisms, percent cover of all sessile organisms or bare rock was estimated in the Boulder Patch in August 2004. Five random point contact surveys (RPCs; Coyer et al. 1999) were conducted along each of eight randomly placed 30 m transects. A RPC is a 1 m bar with a 1.5 m knotted line attached to either end. The line is pulled taught along both sides of the bar and every organism or substrate type that lies directly under each knot is recorded. Ten points are recorded along every RPC bar, each point representing 10% cover. Means of the ten random points on every RPC and subsequent means of all RPCs were used to obtain the average cover for bare rock and the following major taxa: hydroids, bryozoans, sponges, crustose corallines, and red algal holdfasts. Other taxa that were too rare to contribute to the cover estimations included kelp holdfasts, tunicates, spirorbid polychaetes, and soft corals. To determine the major space occupier, coverage of all sessile organisms recorded during the RPCs was compared using a one-way ANOVA and Fisher's PLSD post-hoc test after an arcsin transformation.

To determine which organisms are dominant competitors, overgrowth patterns on Boulder Patch boulders were evaluated in August 2003 and 2004. For this, 157 total boulders were qualitatively examined, on which 449 live interactions were observed (ties and intraspecific interactions were not considered). Erect organisms with small attachments to the rocks were included in the analysis as they still can be important space occupiers, although the base commonly is not the active growing region. For each overlapping border, the overgrown organism was scored "loser" compared to "winner" (the overgrowing organism).

Results

Surveys showed that 60% of the substrate was hard boulders and 40% soft sediments. Of the 60% hard substrate, significant differences were found amongst sessile organism cover (ANOVA, $F_{5,234} = 72.738$, $P \leq 0.0001$, Fig. 1). Only 5.6% of the total hard substrate was bare rock while organisms covered the remaining surface. Crustose coralline algae covered over 60% of the available hard substrate and were significantly more abundant than any other taxon (post hoc

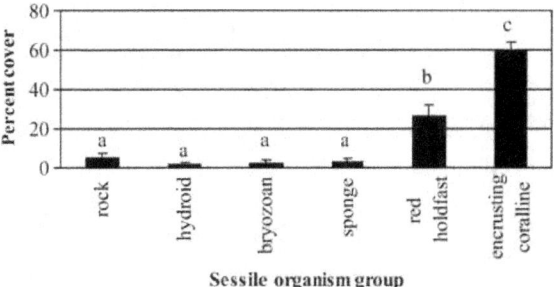

Fig. 1 Mean percent cover (± 1 SE) of rock and various sessile organisms at the Boulder Patch, $n = 40$. Results of post hoc test are indicated by *letters* above *bars* with *different letters* representing significant differences at the 99% level

Fisher's PLSD, $P \leq 0.0001$). Foliose red algal holdfasts covered approximately 25% of the hard substrate, rendering them significantly more abundant than any invertebrate group or bare rock (PLSD, $P \leq 0.0001$). Hydroids, bryozoans, and sponges covered the remaining hard substrate. No significant differences in percent cover were found among invertebrate groups or between invertebrate groups and bare rock.

In the observed 449 competitive border interactions, crustose corallines won only over a few groups of sessile organisms (red algal holdfasts, kelp holdfasts, and hydroids) but lost to most others (tunicates, bryozoans, and sponges; Table 1). Overall, tunicates, upright bryozoans, and sponges were the most frequent winners in border interactions. Sponges won all but one (with an upright bryozoan) out of 70 observed interactions. Upright bryozoans won all their 14 border competitions.

Discussion

Although crustose coralline algae were the major space occupiers in this high Arctic ecosystem, they were not the competitive dominants in many of the interactions with other sessile organisms, particularly invertebrates. This is not unusual as overgrowth dominants often do not monopolize space, and in fact, the most abundant species can be mid-ranked to lower ranked competitors (Airoldi 2000; Barnes and Dick 2000). In our study as well as in other areas, sponges and bryozoans are competitive dominants in inter-phyletic encounters, overgrowing most other organism groups (Nandakumar 1996; Maughan and Barnes 2000; Barnes and Kuklinski 2004). Good competitors in other areas also include spirorbids, polychaete tube mats, and erect hydroids (Sebens 1986). Spirorbids and hydroids had mixed results in this study but were not abundant or competitively superior.

The question remains as to why sponges, bryozoans, and tunicates are not the dominant space occupants, if they are competitively dominant over coralline algae? We observed that most interactions occur on the sides of

Table 1 Mean percent ± 1 SE of the overgrowth scores in the 449 interactions found on boulders

	Crustose corallines	Foliose red algae	Kelp holdfasts	Tunicates	Encrusting bryozoans	Upright bryozoans	Hydroids	Sponges	Spirorbids	Soft corals
Crustose corallines	n/a									
Foliose red algae	2.0 ± 1.5 (73)	n/a								
Kelp holdfasts	9.7 ± 5.4 (31)	n/a	n/a							
Tunicates	95.2 ± 3.3 (21)	n/a	n/a	n/a						
Encrusting bryozoans	87.6 ± 2.7 (89)	93.3 ± 6.7 (15)	n/a	8.33 ± 8.3 (6)	n/a					
Upright bryozoans	100 ± 0 (13)	n/a	n/a	n/a	100 (1)	n/a				
Hydroids	4.2 ± 2.5 (59)	75.0 ± 25.0 (2)	n/a	0 (2)	0 (7)	n/a	n/a			
Sponges	100(39)	100 (22)	100 (1)	100 (1)	n/a	0 (1)	100 (6)	n/a		
Spirorbids	12.2 ± 4.5 (41)	n/a	n/a	n/a	88.3 ± 11.1 (9)	n/a	n/a	n/a	n/a	
Soft corals	100 (3)	n/a	n/a	n/a	n/a	n/a	n/a	n/a	n/a	n/a

Vertical organisms on the left correspond to the winners while organisms across the top correspond to losers. *Numbers* in *parentheses* refer to the observed number of interactions. *n/a* refers to no interactions found

boulder sides while the top or up-facing surfaces are dominated by corallines. High macroalgal abundance on up-facing surfaces is common while sessile invertebrates are abundant on down-facing or vertical surfaces (Irving and Connell 2002). This suggests that there are micro-habitat differences among surface orientations arising from dissimilar conditions (i.e. sediment and light) on the various substrate orientations. Some invertebrates, especially prostrate forms and filter feeders, may experience high mortality in relation to sedimentation from smothering (Duggins et al. 1990). We suggest that sediment load, which is high in the Boulder Patch, may be lethal to many invertebrates, forcing them toward the vertical sides of boulders. In addition, suspended sediments are likely to decrease light intensity through increased turbidity (Ruffin 1998). While invertebrates thrive on shaded surfaces (Baynes 1999; Glasby 1999), macroalgae typically survive better on up-facing surfaces where light intensity is highest (Irving and Connell 2002), resulting in high algal abundance on top surfaces.

Although coralline algae lost most competitive overgrowth battles in this study, they dominated primary substrate. Corallines can survive overgrowth and may even continue to grow while overgrown (Dethier and Steneck 2001). As such, they have been suggested to maintain their abundance in communities until predation or some other disturbance removes the over-grower (Sebens 1986). While the importance of biological disturbance (grazing) in the Boulder Patch community is under current investigation (B. Konar, unpublished data), physical factors such as sedimentation, low light, and wave action, likely have structuring effects on the epilithic community.

Climate change may influence benthic community structure through an alteration of disturbance regimes. A significant loss of Arctic sea ice is predicted to occur by 2025 (Clarke and Harris 2003), particularly in coastal regions (Morison et al. 2000). We suggest that Arctic nearshore systems such as the Boulder Patch would actually experience more disturbances as a result of climate change. Lack of shore fast-ice cover could result in

an increase in wave action and storm surge in these shallow waters. There also could be an increase in sedimentation due to the increase in river discharge caused by melting glaciers, causing further decreasing light levels. This increase in disturbance will probably benefit the crustose coralline community, but be detrimental to most other organisms, likely resulting in communities with fewer species (Barnes and Kuklinski 2004).

Acknowledgments We thank the Dunton Brothers and BP (particularly everyone at Endicott Production Island) for logistical support. We also thank our field assistants: C Debenham, N Harman, and C Wyatt. Helpful comments on a previous draft of this manuscript were provided by C. Belben, B. Daly, C. Debenham, A. Dubois, N. Harman, J. Markis, and T. Spurkland. This project was partially funded by the Coastal Marine Institute.

References

Airoldi L (2000) Effects of disturbance, life histories, and overgrowth on coexistence of algal crusts and turf. Ecology 81:798–814

Barnes DKA (2002) Polarization of competition increases with latitude. Proc R Soc London Series B 269:2061–2069

Barnes DKA, Dick MH (2000) Overgrowth competition in encrusting bryozoan assemblages of the intertidal and infralittoral zones of Alaska. Mar Biol 136:813–822

Barnes DKA, Kuklinski P (2004) Scale-dependent variation in competitive ability among encrusting Arctic species. Mar Ecol Prog Ser 275:21–32

Baynes TW (1999) Factors structuring a subtidal encrusting community in the southern Gulf of California. Bull Mar Sci 64:419–450

Bertness MD, Leonard GH (1997) The role of positive interactions in communities: lessons from intertidal habitats. Ecology 78:1976–1989

Clarke A, Harris CM (2003) Polar marine ecosystems: major threats and future change. Environ Conserv 30:1–25

Coyer J, Steller D, Witman J (1999) A guide to methods in underwater research: the underwater catalog. Shoals Marine Laboratory

Dethier MN, Steneck RS (2001) Growth and persistence of diverse intertidal crusts: survival of the slow in a fast-paced world. Mar Ecol Prog Ser 223:89–100

Duggins DO, Eckman JE, Sewell AT (1990) Ecology of understory kelp environments. II. Effects of kelps on recruitment of benthic invertebrates. J Exp Mar Biol Ecol 143:27–45

64

Dunton KH (1990) Growth and production in *Laminaria solidungula*: relation to continuous underwater light levels in the Alaskan High Arctic. Mar Biol 106:297–304

Dunton KH, Schonberg SV (2000) The benthic faunal assemblage of the Boulder Patch kelp community. In: Truett JC, Johnson SR (eds.) The natural history of an arctic oil field, Chapter 18. Academic Press, NY, pp 371–397

Glasby TM (1999) Effects of shading on subtidal epibiotic assemblages. J Exp Mar Biol Ecol 234:275–290

Irving AD, Connell SD (2002) Sedimentation and light penetration interact to maintain heterogeneity of subtidal habitats: algal versus invertebrate dominated assemblages. Mar Ecol Prog Ser 245:83–91

Jompa J, McCook LJ (2002) Effects of competition and herbivory on interactions between a hard coral and a brown alga. J Exp Mar Biol Ecol 271:25–39

Maughan B, Barnes DKA (2000) Seasonality of competition in early development of subtidal encrusting communities. PSZN Mar Ecol 21:205–220

Morison J, Aagaard K, Steele M (2000) Recent environmental changes in the Arctic: a review. Arctic 53:359–371

Nandakumar K (1996) Importance of timing of panel exposure on the competitive outcome and succession of sessile organisms. Mar Ecol Prog Ser 131:191–203

Ruffin KK (1998) The persistence of anthropogenic turbidity plumes in a shallow water estuary. Estuar Coast Shelf Sci 47:579–592

Sebens KP (1986) Spatial relationships among encrusting marine organisms in the New England subtidal zone. Ecol Monogr 56:73–96